EMILY POST'S
TABLE MANNERS FOR KIDS

Emily Post's
TABLE
MANNERS
for Kids

By Peggy Post
&
Cindy Post Senning, Ed.D.

Collins

An Imprint of HarperCollinsPublishers

Is this still alive?

Emily Post quotation on page 11 from *Etiquette: In Society, in Business, in Politics and at Home*
(New York: Funk & Wagnalls Company, 1922, page 584).
Emily Post is a registered trademark of The Emily Post Institute, Inc.
Collins is an imprint of HarperCollins Publishers.
Emily Post's Table Manners for Kids
Text copyright © 2009 by The Emily Post Institute, Inc.
Illustrations copyright © 2009 by Steve Björkman
Printed in the U.S.A.

Library of Congress Cataloging-in-Publication Data
Senning, Cindy Post.
    Emily Post's table manners for kids / by Peggy Post and Cindy Post Senning. —1st ed.
        p.   cm.
    Includes index.
    ISBN 978-0-06-111709-1
    1. Etiquette for children and teenagers. I. Post, Peggy II. Title. III. Title: Table manners for kids.
BJ1857.C5S46   2009   2008010655
395.5'4083—dc22

Typography by Jeanne L. Hogle
09   10   11   12   13   LP/WOR   10   9   8   7   6   5   4   3   2   1

First Edition

We dedicate this book to the many
kids and adults who have asked us about
how to enjoy their meals with others.
That's the beauty of knowing the basics of table manners:
to be able to relax (that is, not to worry!)
about the dos and don'ts of manners—
and then to focus on the people you're having a meal with.
Enjoy!

—P.P. and C. P. S.

For Mom, who taught me about kindness
and consideration . . . and the importance of using a napkin.

—S. B.

CONTENTS

All the rules of table manners
are made to avoid ugliness. To let anyone see
what you have in your mouth is repulsive,
to make a noise is to suggest an animal,
to make a mess is disgusting.

—*Emily Post on table manners*

CHAPTER ONE

EVERYDAY TABLE MANNERS

T able manners have been included in etiquette books for generations because eating with others has always presented the opportunity to "gross each other out"—and good manners help reduce that risk. But as times change, manners change. Just as there was a time when there were no fast-food restaurants, today we rarely encounter finger bowls and butlers.

Even though the manners have changed, the fundamental principles that govern how we get along with one another never have. Respectful, considerate, and honest behavior *must* be the basis for all our relationships, whether we are meeting someone at a fast-food restaurant, going to a reception, or sharing a meal at home. The manners included in this book are here to help you as you eat and socialize throughout the day—at breakfast, lunch, or dinner. Etiquette will continue to change over time, and someday in the future you may find yourself faced with a new situation for which you don't know the appropriate manners. But if you treat those who are eating with you according to the basic principles of good manners and keep in mind Emily's comment on the ugliness of eating that is quoted at the beginning of this book, you will be okay. So, let's dig in. . . .

FROM SOUP TO DESSERT

Since most table manners evolved to help us keep from grossing each other out, you can see why there are specific manners for specific foods. For instance, the challenges for eating soup are quite different from the challenges for eating spaghetti. In this chapter we'll talk about the manners that go with either specific courses or specific foods.

COMING TO THE TABLE

PICTURE THIS: Your mother gives the call. It's time for dinner. Your sister comes in from outside. She kicks off her sandals, her hands are very dirty, and she still has remnants of her ice-cream cone on her face. You are really grossed out.

Your mother will probably say something to your sister and send her off to clean up before coming to the table. Then, at least, you and the rest of your family will have a better shot at enjoying your meal. The point is this: Table manners really begin *before* the meal.

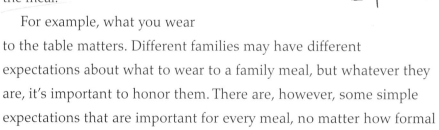

For example, what you wear to the table matters. Different families may have different expectations about what to wear to a family meal, but whatever they are, it's important to honor them. There are, however, some simple expectations that are important for every meal, no matter how formal or informal your family tradition is:

+ Wear a shirt and shoes.
+ Leave your cap behind.
+ If your clothes are dirty, change them.
+ Wash up before coming to the table.

Obviously if you're at a picnic or a barbecue, the shirt and shoes might be left behind and the cap might stay on your head, but cleanliness is important no matter where you are. Not only are dirty hands and fingernails unhealthy, they are definitely nasty for everyone around you to have to look at during the meal.

BEFORE YOU BEGIN EATING . . .

It's important to wait to start eating until everyone is served and you've said grace (if that's the custom).

Do they say grace? Many families start a meal with saying grace, but many do not. If it is not a custom to say grace at your home and you are at a friend's house where they do, sit quietly while they say grace and don't begin eating until you see your friend start. If you have a friend over for the first time and it is your custom to say grace, tell him what to expect as you head for the table: "Hey Jack, I just wanted to let you know that my mom says grace every night before we start eating."

Is everyone seated? Wait until everyone is seated or until your mother, father, or host tells you to go ahead and begin.

While you're waiting, there are a few things you can do. Start by putting your napkin in your lap. Then take a good look at the table. Are there rolls? If so, it's okay to go ahead and take one before dinner is served. It is also okay to take a sip of your water or milk. Check out your table setting (see Chapter Two). It will give you some clues about what you can expect from the meal.

LET'S GET STARTED—
EATING, THAT IS!

Sometimes you have only one course; other times you eat a meal with as many as five courses. You may have a quick lunch and then move on. That would be one course. Perhaps you are at home eating with your family and you enjoy the main course and then a dessert. That would be two courses. Or maybe you're at a formal dinner where you are served five courses: an appetizer, soup, a salad, a main course, and a dessert. That would be *some* meal!

But why not just serve it all at the same time? Food is served in courses to make a meal into an event. A fancy five-course meal is all about eating and celebrating together. The event is intended to take time—maybe hours—and the purpose is to enjoy both the food and the company for the evening. All the courses are planned and prepared to give the diner a great eating experience. The first courses—appetizers, soup and/or salad—are served to give the diners something to whet their appetite for the main course to come. When you're at a restaurant, these courses also take the edge off if you're starving and waiting for your meal. The main course, the premiere act,

---

BREAD AT THE TABLE

1. ***Put one serving on your bread plate,*** *or, if there isn't one, put the bread on your dinner plate. One serving of bread equals:*
   - ✦ *One roll*
   - ✦ *One to three bread sticks*
   - ✦ *One slice*
   - ✦ *One small hunk (broken off the main loaf)*

2. *Put **one serving of butter** on your plate.*

3. *Break off a **bite-sized piece** of bread.*

4. *Hold the bread **between your thumb and forefinger**, not in the palm of your hand.*

5. ***Butter the bread,*** *or dip it in oil if that's what's on the table.*

6. ***Enjoy!***

Food is served in courses to make a meal into an event. . . . The purpose is to enjoy both the food and the company for the evening.

is an entrée and side servings of vegetables and potatoes or rice. The salad can be served after the main course, instead of before it, and then a sweet for dessert can follow. However, more is not necessarily better. The number of courses does not determine whether it is a good meal or not. It is all about the food and the company.

If you do have an appetizer, there are some guidelines to easy eating. They come in all shapes and sizes. Some appetizers you eat with your fingers, some with a fork. Sometimes everyone at the table will have to share one dish. A plate of nachos or dim sum may be placed in the center of the table for

Umm . . . those are nachos.
You can use your fingers.

everyone to enjoy a little. Whether it's a shared appetizer or one on your own plate, portions are meant to be small so that you don't get full. Also, your individual appetizer is usually just one type of food and doesn't have a heavy sauce or gravy.

SOUP—ONLY TWO WAYS TO EAT IT!

No matter where you are in the world, soup is often the first course of your meal. And whether you are in Beijing, New York, Cairo, or Mexico City, there are only two ways to eat it.

1. **With a spoon.** Soupspoons come in all shapes and sizes, but they are all designed to get the liquid and whatever solid food there is in your bowl to your mouth. Whether the soup is hot or cold, there are some basic skills that you can use. They are all designed to help prevent spills—or, if you have a spill, to keep it out of your lap.

The best way to eat soup is to skim your spoon across the top of the soup, away from yourself. If you need to tip the bowl to get those last spoonfuls, tip it away from yourself. Once you have a mouthful of soup on your spoon, lean forward slightly and sip the broth from the edge of the spoon. If there are chunks of food in your soup, put the edge of the spoon on your lip and tip the chunky soup into your mouth. If you put the whole spoon in your mouth, you are more likely to dribble.

HOW DO YOU EAT IT?
FRENCH ONION SOUP

One of the trickiest soups to eat is French onion soup. The melted cheese (and it's stringy mozzarella or Gruyère, at that) sits on top of a slice of French bread that no one can eat in one bite. In order to get to the broth underneath, just take a small amount of cheese onto your spoon and twirl it until the strand forms a small clump. Then press the edge of the spoon against the side of the bowl to cut off the strand of cheese. It is okay to use a knife and fork to cut the cheese and bread. Eat the clump of cheese and bread. If strands of the cheese dangle down to your chin, bite them off cleanly and let them drop into the bowl. Then enjoy the onions and broth.

When you are done, put the spoon on the plate that is under the bowl or cup. If there is no plate, or no room on the plate, leave the spoon in the bowl or mug. Make sure the spoon will not topple out when the waiter comes to clear the table.

2. **By sipping it directly from the mug, cup, or bowl.**

✦ If your soup is served in a mug with a handle you may drink it, as you would drink a beverage.

✦ If your soup is served in a cup, take your cue from the presence of handles. If there are none, use your spoon to eat the soup.

✦ If your soup is served in a large, flat bowl with a rim, you really can't drink from it. But you *can* drink from a smaller bowl if it has a handle on each side.

Whichever container you have for your soup, if you are drinking directly from it, just take one swallow at a time. Also, to get the chunks of meat or vegetables, use your spoon rather than try to slurp them into your mouth directly from the container.

SALAD

A QUESTION *for* CINDY & PEGGY

QUESTION: *I was eating dinner at a friend's house. His mother served a tossed salad with huge lettuce leaves in it. I tried to put a whole leaf in my mouth and wound up with salad dressing all over my face. What could I have done differently?*

ANSWER: *It is okay to cut up a lettuce leaf with your dinner knife (salad knives are rarely used these days). However, don't make a beautiful garden salad look like cole slaw by cutting the entire thing into tiny pieces before you eat the first bite! Cut up a couple of bites or pieces at a time. If your knife is taken away with your salad plate, just ask for a clean one when you get your main course.*

A salad is a great way to start a meal. (Although if you are in Europe, you might find that the salad is served after the main course.) It is often served instead of an appetizer. Just like an appetizer, it can take the edge off your appetite without filling you up so much that you spoil your dinner. And eating a salad gives you something to do while waiting for your main course.

If the salad is served already dressed, you have no choices, but if it is not, you may have several. Sometimes there will be two or three salad dressings on the table. Sometimes separate containers of oil and vinegar may be offered

HOW DO YOU EAT IT?
CHERRY TOMATOES

The trick to eating a cherry tomato is to use your knife or the edge of the salad bowl to hold the cherry tomato steady as you stick a fork into it. Gently push the tines of your fork against the tomato until they puncture it. If the tomato is large, cut it in half by using the holes you just made with your fork as the spot to set the knife. If the tomato is small enough to pop it into your mouth, do so. But . . . be very careful to keep your lips closed as you bite into the tomato so you don't squirt the person sitting next to you.

as well. Each dressing may be in a bottle, in which case you can choose which one you want and pour a small amount from the bottle onto your salad. Or the dressings may be in a gravy boat—a serving dish that has a handle on one side and a lip on the other so you can pour a little of your favorite directly onto your salad. Or, if there is a serving spoon with the gravy boat, go ahead and spoon the amount you want onto your salad. Then mix your dressing into your salad gently with your fork. You should avoid a major toss right there on your salad plate.

AND NEXT—THE MAIN COURSE

The main course is just that. You may or may not have an appetizer, soup, or salad, but you will definitely have a main course. The varieties of main courses are endless, some of which are foods that are typical for each meal. For instance:

+ Eggs, pancakes, or cereal for breakfast.
+ Sandwiches, omelets, and other lighter fare for lunch (or dinner, if you've had a "big" meal for lunch).
+ For the main course of the main meal of the day, a protein, a starch, and one or more vegetables. Pasta dishes such as spaghetti, lasagna, or tortellini may be the main part of the main course.

GETTING YOUR FOOD

A QUESTION *for* CINDY & PEGGY

QUESTION: *Which way should the food be passed around the table when it is first served?*

ANSWER: *Tradition says that you should pass the food in a counterclockwise direction—that is, to your right. (However, it is more important to pass all the dishes in the same direction, so if someone starts out passing the food to the left, the polite thing to do is to follow suit.) Hold the dish for the person on your right while he serves himself, pass the dish to him, and then he should hold the dish for the person on his right and pass it, and so it goes. If you are first, serve yourself a little bit, then start the passing routine or simply wait until the dish makes its way around the table. If the dish is heavy or awkward, place it down on the table with each pass.*

In some homes, the main dishes are brought to the table on platters or in bowls and are placed in front of the person sitting at the "head" of the table, along with a stack of plates. If there are only four or five of you at the table, the host will serve the food onto each plate and everyone will pass that plate around to the right. The first plate should go all the way around the table to the person sitting at the left of the host. Each plate should be passed around until everyone has a plate of food. If there is a large group at the table, the host might suggest how far around to pass the plates and then serve the second half of the table to his left. Sometimes the host can indicate where the plate should go by asking, "Elijah, how hungry are you?" or, "Would you like a little bit of everything?" Whichever way the plates go around, you should wait until everyone has their food to start eating.

Another way food may be served is where a dinner plate is in front of each person and the meal is served from bowls or platters that are set out on the table. Each person spoons a serving onto her plate and then passes the dish to the person on her right. This is called "family style service" and is used in restaurants and resorts as well as in private homes.

As with all meals, it is important to wait until everyone is served unless the hostess suggests you begin eating.

Some families simply serve the food in the kitchen and then everybody brings their meal to the table. When you are the guest you can follow your friend's lead and do as he or she does.

At a formal meal where you do not order individually, the waitstaff serves the food to each diner. The server presents the platter or bowl on your left. You have the option of accepting or refusing the dish. If it is not a food you like, simply say, "No thank you." You do not have to explain or make excuses.

If you order individual meals in a restaurant, the waiter will also serve food to you on your left. As with all meals, it is important to wait until everyone is served unless the hostess suggests you begin eating. In a restaurant, if your dish has not been brought to you, it is considerate to suggest that others begin eating so their food doesn't get cold.

PLEASE PASS THE SALT . . .

Here are some common items on the table that everyone might use:
✦ **Salt and pepper shakers,** which are passed together even if someone has only asked for one of them.
✦ **The bread basket,** which usually holds one portion for everyone at the table. It is important not to take a second or third roll without making sure everyone who wants bread has had a chance to take a piece.

✦ **Butter,** which may be served at individual place settings or on a plate that is passed around to everyone.

If coffee is being served, there will be sugar and milk available for everyone.

Here are some other tips that come up when you are serving yourself. Your first concern is to pay attention to what you are doing and avoid spills. Then, keep these tips in mind:

✦ Spoon sauces or gravy directly from the gravy boat onto the meat, potatoes, or rice that is on your plate.

✦ Put condiments such as mustard or ketchup, pickles, or jelly alongside the food they are meant to accompany.

✦ Put olives, nuts, radishes, or celery on the bread plate or on the side of your dinner plate.

✦ If a dish is beyond an easy reach, even when you're leaning forward slightly, ask someone to please pass it to you. Avoid the "boardinghouse reach," which is leaning across the person next to you or practically lying down on the table to get to something.

✦ Always taste your food before adding any seasoning. Then, if you need it, carefully add the condiment. Otherwise, to hastily cover a dish with salt or drown it in ketchup could imply that you think the food is too bland, which might offend the cook, so keep it light.

IS IT SALT OR PEPPER?

QUESTION: *Sometimes the salt and pepper shakers look exactly alike except for the holes on the top. One will have larger holes, the other smaller. Which is which?*

ANSWER: *The pepper is in the shaker with the larger holes or just one hole.*

Easy now, don't let it fly off the plate!

USING UTENSILS

Cutting your food. If you have meat or fish for the main course, you will most likely have to cut it into bite-sized pieces. Holding the knife and fork the right way will provide you with the most control over the food on your plate. If you hold your fork or knife like a dagger, at the top of the utensil, you will have very little control. If you hold it correctly, you can cut the food into tiny little pieces that you can handle with complete control.

As with any other tools, using a knife and fork correctly takes practice before you can handle them with skill and dexterity.

✦ **Take the fork in your left hand,** with the tines facing down. The handle of the fork should be cupped in the palm of your hand, with your pointer finger on top of the back of the handle, pointing toward the tines.

✦ **The knife should be in your right hand,** with the handle cupped in the palm of your hand and your pointer finger on the back of the blade, right where it attaches to the handle.

✦ **Pierce a section of the meat** that will be bite sized when you cut it off. Then cut with the knife about one-quarter inch from your fork. (If you cut too far away from the fork, the whole piece of meat moves back and forth and may knock other food off your plate.)

✦ **Once you have the right-sized piece** of food on your fork, raise it to your mouth, with the fork tines still down, and eat it.

✦ **If you cut too big a bite**, cut it in half and eat each piece separately.

This is called the Continental, or European, method. It may feel awkward at first, but with practice it actually is very comfortable. The American method starts out just like the Continental method, but the difference occurs when you have finished cutting the meat: You put your knife down at the top of the plate, with the blade facing toward the center of the plate. Then you transfer the fork to your right hand, tines up, and eat the long-awaited bite! Either method is okay. If you are left-handed, the Continental method may be more comfortable for you.

When you eat food that is bite sized or soft enough that you don't need

HOW DO YOU EAT IT?
SPAGHETTI
MULTIPLE CHOICE

a. You twirl several strands around the tines of the fork and use the edge of the plate to brace the fork until you have a bite-sized clump on the fork.

b. You take several strands onto the fork, hold the tines of the fork against the bowl of a dessert-sized spoon, and twirl the fork until the strands are compacted into a bite-sized piece.

c. You cut the spaghetti into bite-sized pieces (one bite at a time) and eat them with your fork.

CORRECT ANSWER:
They are all correct. Use whichever method you feel the most comfortable with.

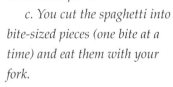

to cut it, you hold the fork like a pencil, not a shovel. Use the hand you write with to pick up the fork. Grasp the fork between your thumb and forefinger in the middle of the handle. The bottom of the handle should be resting on your other three fingers. Scoop up your food, twist the end of the fork with the food on it toward you, and bring the bite to your mouth. The amount of food on your fork should be the size of one comfortable bite. If there is too much food on your fork, it is likely to spill onto your lap.

If your meal is made up of soft foods, you can use the side of your fork to cut them into bite-sized pieces when necessary. If you need help getting the bites onto the fork, hold a piece of bread, or your knife, down onto the plate with your left hand and push the food onto your fork.

A FEW WORDS ABOUT BEVERAGES

Blowing bubbles, gurgling, gulping, or spitting in your beverage can be a source of great amusement. However, remember that this is not acceptable at the dinner table. Any kind of noise at the table other than talking is really quite rude. Here are some tips for "polite" drinking:

+ Instead of chugging the whole drink at one time, take no more than one or two swallows at a time.

+ Swallow the liquid immediately—no

swishing, sloshing, gurgling, or gargling.

◆ Do not blow bubbles in your milk (or any other beverage).

◆ Chew and swallow food before taking a drink.

◆ When a glass or cup is full to the brim, lift it carefully to your mouth and take small, silent sips at the rim until enough liquid is consumed to allow careful drinking. Don't bend over the glass and sip from it while it is resting on the table.

◆ Do not upend or lick the inside of a glass to get the last drop.

In Addition to the Beverage . . .

Lemon wedge. If you have a lemon wedge to flavor your water or other drinks, just squeeze it directly over your beverage. Hold the wedge cupped in your hand or shield it with your other hand so it doesn't squirt onto other people at the table. When you have all the juice out that you want, simply drop the wedge into the glass or cup, or put it on the side of your plate.

Whipped cream. Sometimes hot chocolate and other beverages are served with a delicious mound of whipped cream on the top. Carefully sip the drink from the edge of your cup. If you get whipped cream on the tip of your nose, just use your napkin and wipe it off. Or you can use your spoon and eat the whipped cream and beverage together, just as you would soup.

Sugar. You may want to sweeten your beverage. If the sugar bowl is out of your reach, ask for it. Pick up the sugar bowl and hold it next to your beverage. Put one or two spoonfuls in your glass. Don't use the spoon from the sugar bowl (if there is one) to stir your beverage—you don't want to put a wet spoon back into the bowl. If there is no spoon with the sugar bowl, use your own spoon to scoop the sugar into your glass and stir the beverage. Then, when you have finished stirring, put your spoon on the edge of your plate.

DELICIOUS DESSERTS

A QUESTION *for* CINDY & PEGGY

QUESTION: *What do you do with the dessert fork and spoon that you may find at your place setting?*

ANSWER: *Depending on what you have for dessert, they are interchangeable. Generally, eat custards, puddings, and other soft desserts with your spoon. You eat berries, cakes, cooked fruits (pears or apples, for example), or other firm desserts with your fork. You can eat cake, crepes, or pie à la mode (pie with ice cream) with either your spoon or your fork or both.*

Pie, cake, ice cream, pudding, berries, fruit, or pastries: They are all sweet endings to a meal. They provide temptation for some and are a reward for others. But just because dessert is at the end of your meal doesn't mean it's time to let your manners go. There are a few rules of etiquette that are specifically for eating dessert.

TWO DON'TS FOR ICE CREAM

1. When you have ice cream as a dessert at the table, don't mush it up and make soup out of it.
2. Don't pick up the bowl and drink the ice cream's meltage.

ALL DONE

The meal is over. You have finished eating and you are ready to leave the table. To let everyone know you are finished, put your knife and fork in the four-twenty position on your plate: Line the fork and knife up next to each other, with the tips at the center of the plate and the handles just over the edge of your plate at what would be the four if your plate were a clock. Take care that the utensils are placed so that they will not fall off when you pick up the plate to clear the table.

Here are some additional tips to end meals politely:

◆ Ask to be excused instead of just getting up and leaving.

◆ Wait until there is a natural break in the conversation, so your decision to get up and leave the table is not an interruption.

◆ Put your napkin on the table, take your plate to the kitchen, and push your chair back in under the table.

◆ Offer to help clear the table even if it is not your chore to do so.

◆ And, finally, a thank-you to the cook is in order.

There... four-twenty not three-fifteen. four-twenty on the nose.

CHAPTER TWO

TABLE SETTINGS

There was a time in the distant past when everyone just ate with their hands. They would grab their food and eat it. It must have been pretty gross. As different cultures evolved over time, some developed tools to make eating a little more civilized.

TOOLS FOR EATING

First, **knives** replaced fingers as the way to cut and spear food and then bring it to your mouth. Then, **spoons** were developed to eat liquids and very soft foods.

Forks replaced the spearing-and-carrying part of the knife's job.

Chopsticks were developed to handle food in a way that kept people's hands off it.

Fingers are still the utensil of choice for some foods.

I'm not being rude; I'm being "historical"!

Those cultures where people still eat with their hands have developed specific manners to keep eating a pleasant experience for everyone at the table:

RIGHT HAND ONLY

In the Middle East and in other regions of the world, many foods are still eaten by hand. The most important manner is clear and easy to remember: You handle food with your right hand only, because the left hand is regarded as unclean. This is particularly difficult if you are left-handed, but nonetheless it is very important—so if you are left-handed, practice!

✦ Take your food from the dish at the center of the table, from the side of the dish that is closest to you. Do not reach over the food and grab a piece from the opposite side of the serving platter just because it looks tastier.

✦ Do not touch your lips or teeth with your fingers as you put the food in your mouth.

✦ Lean over your plate a little as you eat, so that any food that spills will land on your plate instead of your lap.

✦ If you need to dip the food into a sauce, break off a bite-sized piece, dip it into the sauce, and pop it into your mouth. Avoid "double dipping"—that is, dipping your food, biting off a piece, and then dipping the rest back into the sauce.

There are some foods you eat with a fork sometimes and with your fingers other times. Which is right? Look at your plate. Do you eat the other foods on the plate with your fingers or a fork? Are the foods covered with sauce or gravy? Also, consider the setting. Are you at a picnic or a formal dinner? Are you with your friends or at your grandmother's house?

SOMETIMES FINGERS, SOMETIMES A FORK

Bacon	**Fingers** *when it is crispy and would break into tiny pieces if you tried to cut it.* **Fork** *when it is limp, thick, greasy, or already broken into small bits.*
Chicken	**Fingers** *when it is fried.* **Fork** *when it is broiled or baked or covered with gravy.*
French fries	**Fingers** *when served with a sandwich or other finger food.* **Fork** *when served as part of a main meal that is eaten with a fork.* **Fork** *when the fries are covered with gravy or ketchup.*
Pizza	**Fingers** *when the pizza can be picked up without too much mess.* **Fork** *when it is really gooey and has lots of toppings piled onto it.* *In either case, you can use a fork to eat any of the food that drops off the pizza onto your plate.*
Shrimp	**Fingers** *when served as an hors d'oeuvre, in a big bowl or on a platter, with a dip.* **Fork** *when served as an appetizer in a small dish, with a shrimp fork.*
Tacos	**Fingers** *when it's a crispy-shell taco. (If you tried to cut it, it would break up and crumble.)* **Fork** *when it's a soft taco. But if there is little or no sauce, you can pick up a soft taco with your fingers to eat it.* *In either case—just as with pizza—you use a fork to eat any of the fillings, soft or crispy, that drop out of the taco onto your plate.*
Watermelon	**Fingers** *when you are eating it outside, or as an informal family dessert.* **Fork** *when you are at a more formal dinner.*

And, if those clues don't give you the answer, what are the other people at your table using? That can be the best clue of all.

Whether you use your fingers or a fork, always come to the table with clean hands and fingernails and keep the following tips in mind:

♦ Make your bites a manageable size.

+ Lean over your plate if there's a risk food might spill out.
+ Use your napkin to clean your fingers and mouth.

THE TABLE SETTING

Utensils were developed to bring some order to eating. Table settings
are also about order. The way the table is set—utensils, plates, glassware,
and napkins—clues you in about which utensils are yours rather than your
neighbor's and which one to use for each course.

The table setting also gives you clues as to what food you can expect
to be served and when. Is there an oyster fork or a soupspoon? Which
fork is on the outside? When you sit down you may see one, two, or three
forks to the left of your plate. You will use them from the outside in, so
if the smaller salad fork is on the outside, you know you will be served
salad before the main course. If it is on the inside, you will have your main

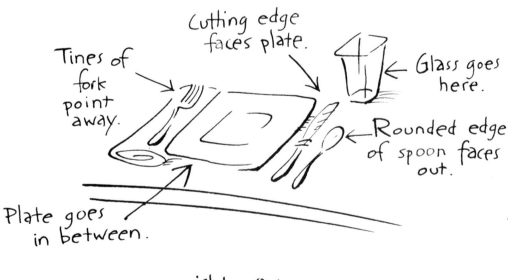

Cutting edge faces plate.

Tines of fork point away.

Glass goes here.

Rounded edge of spoon faces out.

Plate goes in between.

right way

Wrong way

course first. Some tables are set for just one course at a simple family meal. Some are set for a formal, five-course meal. Whichever it is, the basic format is the same no matter how many of each utensil there are and how fancy the tableware is.

THE FAMILY MEAL

The family meal setting provides the basic template. If you learn it, you will always know which items are yours, even at the most crowded table:

Plate. This is the "hub" of the setting and is often the first thing to be set on the table.

Fork. The fork is placed to the left of the plate.

Napkin. The napkin is folded or put in a napkin ring and placed under or to the left of the fork or in the center of the plate.

Knife. The knife is set next to the plate, on the right. The cutting edge should face in, toward the plate.

Spoon. The spoon goes to the right of the knife.

Glass. The drinking glass is placed to the top right of the dinner plate, just above the knife and spoon.

THE THREE-COURSE DINNER

You are likely to see this setting at a fancy restaurant or at parties or receptions where a sit-down meal is served. Since the three-course dinner is preset for all the courses, there will be more utensils by your plate than at the basic family meal. In addition to the basic fork, knife, and spoon, you may have a:

Salad fork, which is smaller than the dinner fork and is set to the left of the plate, next to the larger fork, in the order the salad will be served.

Dessert spoon, which is set to the right of the knife or horizontally above the plate.

Soupspoon, which is at the far right of the setting.

Salad plate, which is to the left of the forks.

Bread plate, which is on your left, just above your forks.

Coffee cup and saucer, which are above and slightly to the right of the knife, with the coffee spoon resting on the right side of the saucer.

Rather than forks, spoons, knives, or fingers, many cultures use chopsticks. If you are not accustomed to using them, it does take some practice, but if you are given chopsticks to use with your meal, give them a try. Often they come in a paper package as two wooden sticks stuck together.

1. Remove the chopsticks from the paper wrapper and break them apart.

2. The top end is usually thicker; the bottom is the narrower end.

3. The bottom, rounded end is the one you use to pick up your food and put it in your mouth. The thicker, top end is used to pick up food from the communal serving plate. Once you use the smaller end to put food in your mouth, it should never touch any bowl or platter used by others.

4. Holding your chopsticks correctly will make all the difference:

a. Rest the lower chopstick on your ring finger, supporting it in the V of the thumb and forefinger.

b. Hold the upper chopstick like a pencil. Rest it between your middle and index fingers and hold it steady with your thumb (it's sort of like holding a pencil).

c. Keep the tips of the chopsticks even.

d. When you pick up your food, the lower chopstick stays still as the upper chopstick moves to hold the food against the lower one.

CHOPSTICKS DOS AND DON'TS

✦ **Do** decide which piece of food you will take from the communal dish and then touch only that piece. Once your chopsticks have touched a piece of food, you must take it.

✦ **Do** bite in half any items that are a little too large to fit comfortably in your mouth, holding the other half firmly with the chopsticks while you bite it.

✦ **Do** raise your rice bowl to your chin when eating rice. The only exception is in Korean dining, where all the dishes remain on the table.

✦ **Do** rest your used chopsticks on your plate or on the chopstick rests—never directly on the table.

✦ **Don't** pour sauce over your food. Instead, use your chopsticks to dip your food into your small bowl of sauce before eating it.

✦ **Don't** grip the edge of a plate with your chopsticks in order to pull it toward you.

✦ **Don't** stand up your chopsticks in your rice. Instead, rest them on the edge of your rice bowl or plate.

Bread plate

Dessert fork and
Dessert spoon (hooray for dessert!)

Salad plate

Salad fork

Soupspoon

THE FORMAL DINNER

Table settings get more complicated as the dinners get more formal. That's because at a formal dinner there are usually three or more courses, and for each course there are different utensils and plates. At a very formal dinner you may have as many as three (sometimes even four) forks, two spoons, three knifes, and four glasses. Which do you use first? As with all meals—whether it's a formal dinner out or a supper at home in the kitchen—start from the outside and work your way in with each course. And if you use your dinner fork to eat your salad and the waiter takes both your forks away, just ask for another dinner fork.

THE ART OF SETTING THE TABLE

Even though there is a template for a table setting, the colors, the designs, and the styles used to decorate the table may be so different, it would be hard to imagine classic table settings are used in every case. But they are! The forks, knives, and spoons will be arranged the same no matter what else is set out with them.

At the center of the table you might see candles. Then again, you might see a flower arrangement. Some people come up with creative centerpieces that give the table a unique look. The centerpiece might match the color of the napkins, or reflect the lace of the tablecloth, or add a completely different dimension. At some formal parties there might be place cards telling you where to sit. The napkins might be folded into some amazing sculpture.

Some utensils are plain; some are ornate. The crystal can be thin and delicate, or it can be thick and chunky. The salt and pepper shakers might be cut glass, or they might be silver. There are so many ways to add to the table setting to create a beautiful, artistic setting. The beauty can only add to the enjoyment of the meal. Simple or fancy, a clean, lovely table is at the heart of a fine meal.

There are so many ways to add to the table setting to create a beautiful, artistic setting. The beauty can only add to the enjoyment of the meal.

CHAPTER THREE

THOSE TRICKIER SITUATIONS

No matter how many books you read, how much you practice, and how good your table manners are, things happen. You could come across a strange-looking food that you have no idea how to eat, or there could be a strange utensil on the table that you have no idea how to use. There is no way you can anticipate everything that you might be served, so learn this general rule of thumb: If you do not know how to eat a certain food on your plate, wait and watch the others at the table. Follow their lead and do what they do.

TRICKIER FOODS?

Sometimes you could be sitting at the table and there, on your plate, is an . . . artichoke. *Uh-oh!* you think. *How do I eat this thing?* Let's think about some of the foods—some common, some unusual—that are not easy to eat.

Artichoke: The artichoke leaves are always eaten with your fingers. Pull the leaf off, dip it in your butter dish, place it between your front teeth, and pull forward, scraping the "meat" off the leaf with your teeth. Continue leaf by leaf, discarding the leaves on the edge of your plate or on the "debris plate" if one is provided. When you reach the thistle-like "choke" at the center of the artichoke, you use your knife to slice off the remaining leaves and the choke and expose the "heart." Cut the heart into bite-sized pieces and use your fork to dip it into your butter dish and then eat it.

Asparagus: When asparagus stalks are firm and there is no sauce on them, you can pick them up with your fingers. However, if you are a guest at a formal meal and no one else is using their fingers, you might want to follow suit and use your knife and fork.

Bacon: See Chapter Two, page 35.

Baked potatoes: When the whole, unskinned potato is served on your plate, just slit the top lengthwise, push on each end of the potato to open the slit wide, and mash the potato with your fork a little at a time. You can also simply cut the potato in half lengthwise and eat the inside of the potato in pieces instead of mashing it. Either way, you can add butter, salt, pepper, sour cream, chives, or other toppings, mash them into the potato, and take a bite directly from the shell. Or you can scoop the potato out of the skin onto your plate, neatly move the skin to the side of your plate, and mix whatever you are adding to the potato with your fork. If you like to eat the skin, cut the whole potato into bite-sized pieces, one or two at a time.

Berries: Berries that have been hulled or have had the stems taken off—and are served with cream—are eaten with your spoon. If strawberries are served unhulled, it is fine to pick up the berry by the stem, eat it (sometimes in more than one bite), and leave the hull and leaf on the side of your plate.

Bread: See Chapter One, page 16.

Bruschetta: For an appetizer you may be served bruschetta, which is Italian bread with a tomato topping. It may just involve picking up the toasted bread with your fingers, carefully bringing it to your mouth, and biting off a piece without spilling the tomatoes or crunchy crumbs all over yourself. (The only trick is to do it carefully while leaning over your plate.)

Or it may come in a large piece with the bread still soft enough to cut into bite-sized pieces with your knife, and then use your fork to lift the bite-sized piece to your mouth. In either case, use your fork to eat the tomatoes that fall off the edges onto your plate.

Buffalo wings: If you are sharing the blue cheese dip with others at the table, spoon a small amount onto your plate—or onto the buffalo wing itself, leaving the end that you will pick up with your fingers clean. Then pick up the clean end of the wing with your fingers, eat it as carefully as you can, then wipe your fingers and lips with your napkin.

Gee, for such big animals, buffaloes sure have tiny wings!

Cherry tomatoes: See Chapter One, page 21.

Clams: Clams may be served with an oyster fork, in which case you hold the shell between your thumb and forefinger and use your fork to eat the clam. If there isn't a fork, you pick up the clam between your thumb and forefinger and slide the clam directly into your mouth.

Corn on the cob: The trick to eating corn on the cob is to be as neat as possible. Put pats of butter on your plate and then use your knife to butter a few rows of corn at a time. Then take just a bite or two at a time rather than chomp back and forth along the rows like an old-fashioned typewriter. One practice in some families is to roll the ear of corn onto a stick of butter that is used only for that purpose. In that case, be careful not to roll your fingers in the butter, too. If you don't know what the routine is at the table where you are served corn on the cob, just watch the other diners and follow along.

Fajitas: You fill and roll your own fajita and then eat it with your fingers. To keep things neat, spread any soft fillings onto the tortilla first, then add the strips of meat and peppers and whatever you are having, top with any garnishes, fold in the bottom of the tortilla, roll it up, and eat from the open end. Use your fork to eat any filling that drops out onto your plate.

Fondue: The most important thing to be aware of when eating fondue is to NOT "double dip." When you eat fondue, you are sharing the bowl with everyone else at the table, so you don't want part of your food that has touched your mouth to touch the hot oil or cheese that others will share.

+ **For cheese fondue:** Spear a piece of French bread, dip it into the pot of melted cheese, hold the fondue fork still in order to let the excess drip off, then use your dinner fork to slide the cheese-covered piece onto your plate and eat it.

+ **For meat fondue:** You first take several pieces of the raw meat from a bowl and put them onto your plate. Then, using your fondue fork, place one piece of meat in the pot next to other diners' forks. When your meat is cooked, take it out of the hot oil, let it drip, then put it onto your plate. When it is cool enough, use your dinner fork to eat it.

French fries: See Chapter Two, page 35.

French onion soup: See Chapter One, page 19.

Gravy and other sauces: Is it okay to use your bread to sop up the gravy or the sauce that is left on your plate? Yes, but it's not okay to use your fingers. Put a bite-sized piece of bread into the gravy or sauce and then eat it, using your fork.

Lobster: Eating lobster is so messy, you will probably be given a bib or a large napkin to tuck under your chin. If so, use it, as there are likely to be splashes and squirts and dripped butter throughout the meal! Use the cracking tool that is typically provided, crack each claw, and pull out the meat with a fork or a small lobster pick. Remove the meat from the tail and cut it into bite-sized pieces. Spear each piece of meat with your fork, dip it into your butter dish, and then enjoy! Some people even like to pull each leg off the lobster, put the open end into their mouth, and squeeze the meat out with their teeth for an extra little tidbit. A large bowl or platter should be available for the empty shells. If you're eating lobster in a restaurant, finger bowls or disposable towelettes are usually provided to clean your fingers after the meal.

Melons: When you are served slices of melon at a picnic or an informal meal, just pick up your slice with your fingers and enjoy it. At a more formal affair, use your fork. Carefully flick any seeds off the fruit with the tines of the fork, push them to the side your plate, and then use the edge of the fork to cut the melon into bite-sized pieces.

Peas: Despite every cartoon to the contrary, the correct way to eat those pesky peas is to scoop them up with your fork—you do not try to line them up on your knife. You do not "borrow" your dessert spoon. You do not spear them one by one with your fork. You just slip your fork under the edge of the serving of peas on your plate and *carefully* lift the peas to your mouth.

Pizza: See Chapter Two, page 35.

Sandwiches: If your sandwich is more than an inch thick, cut it into halves or quarters before picking it up. Hold your sandwich with the fingers of both hands to eat it. You always use a knife and fork to eat a hot, open-faced sandwich that is covered with gravy or sauce.

Shish kebob: When shish kebobs are served as an hors d'oeuvre— finger food at a party—or appetizer, you can eat the meat and vegetables directly from the skewer. When they are served as a main course, you use your fork to slip the food off the skewer onto your plate. Put the empty skewer on the edge of your plate and use your knife and fork to cut the meat and vegetables into manageable pieces, one bite at a time.

Hey! It's a meal on a sword!!!

Shrimp: See Chapter Two, page 35.

Spaghetti: See Chapter One, page 27.

Tacos: See Chapter Two, page 35.

WHAT DO I DO WITH . . .

A QUESTION *for* CINDY & PEGGY

QUESTION: *I was at a fancy meal at my friend's house and they had a fruit salad that had cherries in it. When I bit down on a cherry, it had a pit in it. What should I have done?*

ANSWER: *Olives, cherries, some prunes, and some grapes may be served with their pits still in them. If you get a pit in your mouth, you can do one of two things. Move the pit to the front of your mouth with your tongue and just take it out of your mouth with your thumb and forefinger and put it on the edge of your plate. (If it is an olive from an antipasto dish at the center of the table and you don't have a plate in front of you, just put the pit on the edge of your bread plate.) Or, you can bring your fork to the edge of your mouth and gently put the pit on the fork and lower it to your plate. What you don't want to do is spit the pit out onto your plate or into the palm of your hand or your napkin.*

DIFFERENT THINGS ON THE TABLE

With so many different foods, menus, and table settings out there, you are likely to come upon some unfamiliar items. How you handle them will affect how comfortable you are during the meal. For instance, you may be at a formal dinner where the salt is served in a "saltcellar." This is a tiny dish filled with salt. There may be a tiny spoon with it, or no spoon at all. If there is a tiny spoon, simply put a little salt on the spoon and sprinkle it on the food you want to season. If there is no spoon, you can use the tip of a clean knife to take a little mound of salt, place it on the edge of your plate, and dip your food into it. If the saltcellar is for your use only, you may take a small pinch of salt between your thumb and forefinger and sprinkle it where you want it.

Ketchup, mustard, and other condiments are often served in small dishes set out on the table. There should be a small serving spoon with the dish; use the spoon to move a small amount of the condiment onto the side of your plate. Either dip the food (e.g., French fries and ketchup) into that condiment, or use your knife to spread the condiment on your food (e.g., mustard on your meat). As always, you don't want to dip your food directly into a shared dish, or spoon a huge amount of the condiment directly onto your food. A condiment is supposed to enhance the flavor of the food, not drown it out.

TABLEWARE ON THE TABLE

You are eating in a restaurant and don't have a salad, but there is a salad fork at your place. Should you put that unused fork on your dinner plate when you are done?

No. You can just leave unused utensils on the table.

BUT: Whether you are in a restaurant or at home, never put a used utensil down on the table. *Leave any used utensils on your plate or in your bowl.*

PICTURE THIS: You are at a formal dinner, and after the main course the waiter brings out a small glass bowl with a flower or a lemon slice floating in it. There is no spoon. What do you do?

You have just been given a "finger bowl." It is meant for you to delicately wash the tips of your fingers. Just dip the ends of your fingers (one hand at a time) into the bowl, wriggle them around a little, take them out off the water, let the excess water drip off back into the bowl, and, finally, dry your fingertips off on your napkin. The whole thing should only take you a matter of seconds. When finished, you lift the finger bowl and the little doily it comes on and move them to the upper left side of your place setting. Don't forget—when in doubt you can always watch what your host does and then follow suit.

WHAT TO DO WHEN . . .

NO MANNERS FOR CHOKING

If you are choking on your food, you do not need to worry about manners. If you need a drink of water, by all means take it. If that doesn't work, cover your mouth and give a good cough. If you have to cough more than once or twice and you are able to get a good breath, excuse yourself and leave the table.

If food is caught in your throat and you are not able to cough or get a good breath, DO NOT go off by yourself. Do whatever is necessary to get fellow diners to come to your aid. Thankfully, many people (and most restaurant personnel) are trained to perform the lifesaving Heimlich maneuver—a technique that anyone could benefit from learning.

You spill something: You are sitting at a table with seven other people. The table is quite crowded. You reach for the bread basket and you knock over your water glass. The water is running down the table, heading right for your neighbor's lap! What can you do?

It really is quite simple. You put your napkin right onto the spilled water as quickly as you can so that it doesn't reach your neighbor's lap. Then you let the waiter or host know about the spill so they can help you wipe it up. At a formal dinner, the waiter will clean it up. At someone's home or at a more informal dinner, you should offer to help clean up the mess.

ALLERGIES

1. **If you think** you have eaten something you are allergic to and are having a reaction, do tell your host or the waiters.

2. **When you have** a food allergy, it is not only acceptable but is very important to ask about ingredients used in the preparation of the food.

You cough or sneeze: If you have to cough or sneeze, it is best if you leave the table. Sometimes, however, you will not have time. You might find yourself choking on a piece of food, causing you to suddenly cough. Or a sneeze can appear out of nowhere. Your only option in these situations is to turn your face away from the food, cover your mouth or nose, and be as discreet as possible. If you feel another sneeze or cough coming on, excuse yourself and leave for the restroom.

A QUESTION *for* CINDY & PEGGY

QUESTION: *I had just finished enjoying a good meal. I was quite full. I opened my mouth to say something and a loud burp came out. What should I have done?*

ANSWER: *The only thing you could do at that point is say, "Excuse me!" And then move on.*

However, do keep in mind that usually you can control a burp. If that air is already on its way up and out, close your mouth and let the burp out quietly. If a loud burp escapes you and another is on its way, take extra care that the next one is silent. That is how you show consideration for the people you are dining with.

You need to blow your nose: This one is simple: *Never blow your nose at the table!* Leave the table, blow your nose in the restroom, and return when you are finished.

You find something that doesn't belong in your food: "There's a fly in my soup!" You are all set for your first bite of delicious soup. You look down and there is a fly swimming across the bowl. Quietly and without fanfare, simply mention to the waiter or your host that there is something in your soup. It is perfectly reasonable that you might not want to eat the soup after it's had a fly in it, so you should ask for another bowl.

Just as awkward is the situation when you wind up with something in your mouth that you realize doesn't belong there. It could be: a bite of fat, or gristle from meat; a piece of bone; or a hair. Or it could be something you are allergic to (and didn't realize was in the dish).

For all of these you would want to get them out of your mouth. You can quietly take the foreign object out of your mouth with your fingers and put it

You can quietly take the foreign object out of your mouth with your fingers and put it on the edge of your plate. That is better than putting it in your napkin since you might inadvertently rub it onto your face the next time you wiped your mouth.

on the edge of your plate. That is better than putting it in your napkin since you might inadvertently rub it onto your face the next time you wiped your mouth. You should be as discreet as possible and only call the waiter or your host's attention to it if you need a fresh serving or if you think you may have an allergic reaction.

Too much spice or too hot: In these two instances you might just be able to take a sip of water, swallow the food, and then act accordingly. Wait for the food to cool if it was too hot. If it was too spicy, simply leave that food on your plate.

A QUESTION *for* CINDY & PEGGY

QUESTION: *I was at my friend's house for dinner. I love spaghetti, so I served a big helping and then found out the sauce was so spicy, I couldn't eat it. Should I have said something?*

ANSWER: *This is a time for honesty. You can say, "Oh, my goodness, this is much spicier than I am used to. I don't mean to be rude, but I'm not sure if I can finish it." Then eat all the other things on your plate, enjoy a good conversation with your friend, and consider it a lesson learned. The next time, just serve yourself a medium helping so you won't be wasting food if you find you don't care for it. You can always go back for seconds if you find out it's fantastic.*

If you are in a restaurant and think the food has been overly spiced by mistake, you can call it to the waiter's attention and ask for another serving. Do pay attention to the indicators on menus regarding spiciness. If you order something with four peppers next to it, you really should not complain about how hot it is.

CHAPTER FOUR

MEALS ARE SOCIAL EVENTS, TOO!

You need fuel to continue running all day, just like a car does. If meals were only a matter of refueling, you could simply pull up to the "gas" station, refuel (proteins, vitamins, starch, and minerals), and be on your way. How boring! Fortunately, meals are primarily a social event, not just a pit stop.

EVERY DAY; EVERY WEEK

Breakfast: This really has become a meal on the run. You grab a piece of toast, drink some juice, and eat an apple on your way out the door. However, on a weekend, even breakfast can be a special meal when family and friends all sit down to a stack of pancakes, maple syrup, bacon or sausage, juice, hot chocolate, and a dish of fruit. There is time to share plans for the day and to figure out who will be where when.

Lunch: Even in the midst of your busy schedule it's important that you take time to eat and to greet those who eat with you—whether friends in school or your mom at the kitchen table. It is more likely that you'll be at home for lunch on the weekends. However, as more and more things are scheduled during busy weekends, you might find yourself at a fast-food restaurant or a snack bar, or eating from a brown bag when you are off on an all-day event.

Dinner: With the busy schedules that have become the norm today, it seems there are fewer evenings where everyone in the family sits down together at the same time, but the best opportunity for this to happen is still at dinner. Weekends provide the opportunity to go over to a friend's house for dinner or to have a friend over—or perhaps on the rare occasion where you'll be having dinner at your teacher's or at your parent's friend's house. Think of it as great practice for the times in the future when you might be meeting the family of someone who has become really special in your life. In any case, weekends provide the opportunity for social events, and dinner may be the center of the event.

ONCE A YEAR; ONCE IN A LIFETIME

Birthdays: These come but once a year, and in many families the birthday dinner is chosen by the person whose birthday it is. You get to select your favorite foods, perhaps have dinner as the main event at a birthday party, and share the time with your most favorite family and friends.

All meals have a social aspect that is as important as the nutrients you ingest.

Holidays: Think about Thanksgiving. Even 350 years ago, the meal was the focus of an event celebrating the growth of a new community. Families come together around a turkey and mashed potatoes every year on the last Thursday of November. Across the United States, Independence Day is celebrated every July 4 with fireworks and food. In China, the Moon Cake Festival is also celebrated with fireworks and delicious holiday fare. Every culture and religion has special days that mark events people want to commemorate. These are times when families and friends gather together to share history or traditions and often a special meal together.

Weddings and other life events: First comes the ceremony, where the couple actually gets married, and then there is often a reception with a buffet or a seated meal. Wedding anniversaries are marked by special meals with families and close friends. Funerals may be followed by receptions or buffets where people can find comfort just by sharing food. Parties honoring bar and bat mitzvahs often include a special dinner. And on it goes. The list can be endless.

Whether you are sitting in the cafeteria where you eat five days a week or are at that once-in-a-lifetime special celebration, more is happening than simply satisfying your hunger. All meals have a social aspect that is as important as the nutrients you ingest. And there are many things you can do to make every mealtime a social event that works for everyone at the table.

The table setting and the nutritional needs are the mechanics and science of a meal; the social aspects are the art of the meal. The beauty of the table setting, the skill of food preparation, the presentation of each dish, and the conversation of the diners are all part of the art of mealtime. Everyone who eats at the meal has some responsibility for that art, and the manners that have evolved around eating socially can help you approach every meal with confidence. There are a few simple guidelines that will help make every mealtime event one that feeds your social needs as well as your physical hunger.

WHO SITS WHERE?

A QUESTION *for* CINDY & PEGGY

QUESTION: *I was the first one into the room where we were going out to eat. How could I know where I was supposed to sit?*

ANSWER: *It may be quite simple.*

*1. **Look to see if there are place cards.** If there are, find yours and sit there. It is not okay to switch place cards around. Someone has spent some time figuring out who might have a good time sitting next to whom, and one switcheroo could wreck the whole plan.*

*2. **Ask the host or hostess where you should sit.** If you are told to take a specific seat, you should honor that suggestion.*

*3. **Sit where you please** if the host or hostess does not tell you where to sit.*

... more gruel please?

MORE, PLEASE!

Is it polite to ask for seconds? Of course! Nothing is a greater compliment to the chef than having someone ask for more. It may be that all the food was served on the first go-around, so you may not get seconds, but it never hurts to ask.

WHEN YOU DON'T LIKE SOMETHING . . .

Sometimes you will be served a food that you have never seen before or that you have tried before and didn't like. What do you do? It's easy.

+ **Don't spread it around** and try to make it look like you ate it.

+ **Don't force yourself** to eat something that makes you gag.

+ **Don't say "yuck"** or make other negative comments.

+ **Do take a taste** of it, in case the cook has prepared this food in a way that you might like.

+ **Do just leave the food** on the side of your plate if you don't like it.

+ **Do find something positive** to say about the meal if someone asks you.

THE ART OF CONVERSATION

Learning which fork to use, which glass is yours, or where to put your napkin at the end of the meal is pretty straightforward. You can learn it quickly. Knowing what to say, talking to someone you don't know well, or figuring out how to change the subject can be more difficult. You have to practice, practice, practice. One of the reasons it's good to have some of those routine meals at home on a regular basis is to practice managing a good conversation and eating at the same time.

Is this still alive?

REVIEW THE BASICS
MAGIC WORDS

Pass the salt and pepper, please.
Thank you.
You're welcome.
Be polite and everyone will enjoy their meal that much more!

TOP TWELVE TIPS FOR TABLE TALK

1. **Look at the person you are speaking to.**

2. **When you are eating, focus on getting the food to your mouth** first, chewing, and swallowing—then talking.

3. **Talk to people on either side of you or across the table.** Don't shout to people farther down the table.

4. **Don't just talk to one person** if there are others at the table. When you are at a friend's house, talk to her parents or siblings, too.

5. **Show an interest in what people are saying.** Maintain good eye contact, make comments, and answer questions.

6. **Take care to not interrupt.**

7. **Speak clearly.**

8. **Do not talk with your mouth full.**

9. **Avoid gross or sensitive topics.** You don't want to wind up in an argument with someone at the table.

10. **Stay clear of offensive language.**

11. **Say something positive about the meal.** Don't complain about the food.

12. **When you are finished eating, ask to be excused,** offer to help clear the table, and remember to thank whoever prepared

the food and hosted the meal.

If it were only as simple as learning the top twelve tips, you could be the social hit of every occasion. However, just as with any art, there are techniques that help you develop these skills. When you are at dinner with family and friends you may not see often, you might feel a little shy about starting up a conversation. But with a little anticipation and practice, you can master two conversational skills that will ease the awkwardness.

SMALL TALK

Small talk is just what it sounds like. This is not deep conversation about feelings and personal philosophy. Your conversations with close friends and family may have more depth, but with people you don't know well or don't see often, you are at more of a "getting to know you" level. Even with family and close friends, you may want to keep the conversation at a meal on the lighter side. Nothing can spoil a great Thanksgiving dinner quicker than an argument about politics or religion.

The key to getting good at small talk is anticipation. For instance, you know you are going with your friend to her grandmother's house for dinner. Some of her cousins will be there also. You don't know them very well, so you will want to prepare in advance.

+ **Read the newspaper for the week before the dinner. Make special note of any interesting news:**
    ⬧ Has there been a weather-related story that would be easy to talk about?
    ⬧ Has a famous person visited your town recently?
    ⬧ Was there a good human interest story—about pets or kids doing some special project?
+ **Ask your friend about her grandmother:**

◇ Does she have a favorite sports team?

◇ Has she traveled anywhere recently?

◇ Does she have hobbies?

✦ **Be prepared to ask people about their opinions:**

◇ Do they like that new building going up downtown?

◇ Did they see the musical at the high school? What did they think?

✦ **Listen. Listen. Listen.** Other people at the table may be skilled at small talk and you can easily respond to their opening comments.

✦ **Practice. Practice. Practice.** If your sister has a friend over, make some small talk. If you are in a store, ask a salesperson for his opinion on the items you are buying. If you go to your own grandmother's house, ask her about her favorite sports team.

SAFE TOPICS

So what are safe dinner topics that are not apt to create difficult situations?

✦ Sports and sports personalities

✦ Current popular television shows, music, and films

✦ Weather

✦ Local arts events

✦ Special school programs

✦ Travel

✦ Seasonal events

CONTROVERSIAL TOPICS

Sometimes the conversation ends up moving away from small talk. Your friend's cousin makes a negative comment about the fact that the new mayor is a woman. You see no problem with a woman holding a high political office. This could easily get out of hand. The cousin pushes the point. What can you do?

✦ **Be careful to stick to issues and facts that you know.** Facts should be the basis of any response you choose to make. Perhaps you have done a report on the topic of women in politics and have some facts at hand.

✦ **Talk about the subject without offending.** Avoid making it personal. You really don't want to say "That's the dumbest thing you could say" or "How can you be so stupid?"

✦ If you think the conversation is becoming personal or offensive,

curb your inclination to respond.

✦ **Remember: Don't argue**—it's tough to argue when the other person refuses to rise to the bait. That's how you can avoid an argument.

TRICKY SOCIAL ISSUES AT THE TABLE

PICTURE THIS: It's the family Christmas dinner. You are seated next to your great-aunt Consuela. She is telling you the same story about how sad the end of her favorite movie is. You have heard about this same movie year after year and you are so bored. What should you do?

This may be the one day of the year Consuela gets to see her family. She probably doesn't realize she has told you this story many times before, and it is giving her great delight to tell it to you. It may be that you can make her day by listening and commenting. Since you know she is likely to tell this story, be prepared to take it a little bit further. "So, Tía Consuela, what would have made this a happier movie for you?"

Or: Your cousin comes to dinner with her new fiancé and his nine-year-old son. At dinner his son just sits picking at his food and does not seem comfortable joining in the conversation. Remember your newfound skills at small talk. Perhaps you could ask him where he goes to school, or if he plays any sports. Now you have a clue.

Maybe he has said he plays baseball. You can ask him if he has a favorite professional team. Whether you love the same team or find you support rival teams, you now have a lively topic of conversation and you both may enjoy the dinner even more.

CHAPTER FIVE

SPECIAL MEALS

So far we've talked mostly about meals that are served at a table in someone's home or in a restaurant. And most of your meals will be just as we've described. However, there are many meals that don't happen as a "sit down and be served"–type event.

WHEN THE FOOD MUST BE FAST

You walk into a restaurant or perhaps a school cafeteria. There are tables and chairs on one side, a counter with cash registers on the other. The menu is emblazoned on signs above the counter. In front of each register, lines of people wait to place and pay for their order. There are no waiters; the tables have no place settings; small counters along the walls hold condiments,

"LINE" MANNERS

There are definite manners for waiting in line. They all are related to one basic rule: Be patient.

+ **Do not jump from line to line.** *If you discover that the person in front of you is ordering for a whole group, you may move over to the next line, but don't keep switching.*

+ **Do not invite your friends to cut** *in front of or behind you.*

+ **Choose one line.** *Sometimes it might seem that you could stand in one line and your friend in the other and then whoever gets to the counter could order first for both of you. Be aware that others in the lines are apt to find this really annoying.*

+ **Be ready to order when you get to the counter.** *Make good use of your line time to decide what you want.*

+ **If you have to wait for something** *you have ordered to be made, stand to one side so the next person in line can get his order in.*

+ **If you order for several people,** *ask one of them to help you carry things to the table.*

napkins, plastic cutlery, and soda dispensers. And by all the exits there are trash containers topped with shelves just the right size for trays.

Clearly this is not the typical setting for a meal we've been writing about, but just because it is "fast" food doesn't mean you leave common courtesies at the door. It is just as important to speak in a friendly voice with a smile when you order from someone at a cash register as it is when you order from a waiter. Being loud or boisterous is just as irritating to others in a fast-food restaurant as it is in a fancy establishment. The same manners that apply to any meal apply here. For instance, use a napkin to wipe your mouth, chew with your mouth closed, don't play with your food, eat really messy foods with your fork—even though it may just be made of plastic. All the manners that you know can help make the meal more pleasant for those around you. They are important regardless of the setting.

There are several other important things to consider at the fast-food restaurant. Probably the top of the list is to pick up after yourself. Part of the idea behind the fast-food restaurant is that you don't need a big staff to manage it. In order for this to work, everyone has to contribute by leaving a clean table.

PICTURE THIS: You have a tray full of food, all the tables are full except one, and that one is covered with trash. Now you have to put down your tray on a dirty table and clear someone else's mess before you can enjoy your own meal. How does that feel?

If you spill something just on the table, use a napkin and clean it up! If you spill a whole drink on the floor, let someone on the staff know so they can help mop it up. It can be dangerous if you just leave it, as another person could easily slip and fall on a wet floor. And spilled soda that has dried becomes really sticky. It leaves everyone who steps on it feeling the restaurant is dirty and not a great place to eat, when that may not be the case.

And, finally, if the restaurant is crowded, move on when you are finished. The fast-food restaurant is not meant to be a place you sit and linger. Others may be waiting for a table. The whole idea is to come in, eat, and leave. Of course, in the middle of the afternoon, when there might be plenty of empty tables, you don't have to rush along. Just be considerate of others.

THE FOOD COURT

In malls, airports, and other public places you will see the food court. There may be five or six different fast-food restaurants in a semicircle around a large number of tables and chairs. You go to one that serves pizza, your friend prefers hamburgers, and your father really likes Chinese. All the manners that you would use in one fast-food restaurant apply here. The *only* difference is that you all may be eating very different foods. The one basic table manner that does *not* apply here is when to start. At a dinner table you should wait until everyone is seated or served or the hostess tells you to go ahead and eat. At the food court you can start eating when you get to your table, since someone else in your group may be in a long line.

THE SCHOOL CAFETERIA

Another place you frequently eat a meal that is not the typical table meal at home is the school cafeteria. It is important to consider how you can make the school lunch a relaxing break in your hectic school day. Often you only have twenty minutes to get through the line, eat, clean up, and move out. With time pressures, long lines, and crowding, your lunch can add to your daily crunch rather than provide the good break that you need.

There are some things you can do to reduce the risk of total chaos in the cafeteria:

✦ **Make room for others at your table,** even if they are not your best friends.

✦ **Hold your food tray with both hands.**

✦ **Do not take or touch food on someone else's tray** without permission.

✦ **Don't offer to trade food.** This can be awkward if you ask someone who doesn't want to trade.

✦ **Don't make comments** about another student's food.

✦ **Follow the directions** of the adult in charge, even if he is not your teacher.

✦ **Follow basic good behavior** in lines.

✦ **Be respectful** of the servers in the cafeteria line.

✦ **Clear your place** at the table and take your tray to the drop-off station at the end of your lunch period.

FAST FOOD IN THE CAR

*S*ometimes you want your fast food so fast, you don't even get out of the car. A few tips for eating in the car may reduce the risk of spilling and making a mess:

✦ *When you open the wrapper on your food, spread it out on your lap so it's sort of like a plate.*

✦ *If there's no cup holder, try to find a stable place to set down your drink.*

✦ *Keep the lid on your drink and use a straw.*

✦ *Use the bag your food came in for trash. Put the empty ketchup packet, the salt and pepper packets, or the straw wrapper in the bag. When you are finished, wrap up anything left over in the paper on your lap and put it in the bag, too.*

While these tips may seem obvious, they are nonetheless important. If you neglect them and food spills, the car will smell like your fast-food lunch for days to come.

AT A "SIT-DOWN" RESTAURANT

While all the table manners we've talked about apply to all "sit-down" meals, there are a few extra tips for a restaurant meal that are important to keep in mind. When you go to a restaurant for a sit-down meal, you will have the opportunity to look over the menu, order what you like, have someone else serve and clear the table, and enjoy a pleasant evening talking with others. At a restaurant, remember that everyone else is there to have a special time too. The choices you make may very well affect how they will enjoy their meal. These seven tips can help make dining out a pleasure for you, the people you are with, the staff, and the other customers:

1. **All the table manners** that you use at home apply in a restaurant as well.

2. **Your attitude will affect the others with you.** Even if you want to be at home watching the play-off game, you should concentrate on enjoying the meal and then get home for the second half.

3. When you place an order, or even when you're pointing out a problem, **be respectful of the waiter.**

4. Keep in mind that the waiter probably has several tables she is managing and **you may need to wait a few minutes for her attention.**

5. **Ask to be excused** if you need to go to the restroom.

6. **Do NOT use your cell phone** or any other electronic devices at the table. Turn it off before you sit down to your meal. If your cell phone rings (or vibrates) and you must take the call, excuse yourself from the

Hold that thought, Mr. Mayor. It's my pal Mike calling.

table, go to the lobby or front entrance, keep it short, and return to the table.

7. When you leave the table for any reason, **push your chair in** so waiters and other customers can easily get by it.

Many students now eat both breakfast and lunch in the school cafeteria, and the staff are serving food nonstop during the school day. It can be crowded and chaotic. A good meal sets the tone for the rest of the day, so it is important to show respect and consideration for everyone sharing the lunchroom with you.

AT A PICNIC

What could be a better combination than a sunny day, a park or beach, your friends and family, and great food spread out on a blanket or towel? There is something special about a picnic. The food can be as simple as a sandwich and chips with milk or as fancy as a shrimp salad with croissants and sparkling

---

FRIENDS AND FOOD
MULTIPLE CHOICE

It is the first week of school. This year you and your best friends have very different schedules. When you get to the cafeteria for lunch, you realize you don't know anyone well. You could:

a. Find a place to sit, eat your lunch, and leave as quickly as possible.

b. Sit by yourself and read a book while you eat.

c. Find a place to sit, introduce yourself to the other kids at the table, and practice your small talk as you eat.

d. Complain to your teacher that you have no one to sit with.

Other kids might think you are unfriendly if you just eat and leave, or read a book rather than talk with anyone. Complaining to your teacher will probably result in no change. The way you will wind up with friends—or at least lunch mates—will be to get to know some of the kids who share your schedule. So option c has the best chance of speeding that process along.

---

punch. Either way, this is the time you get to eat with your fingers—in a bathing suit, barefoot, or with your baseball cap on.

Picnics are basically informal and are associated with fun. As with every meal, however, your actions should be governed by consideration for others.

No one wants to see your chewed-up hot dog with mustard, so wait until you swallow it to talk. Ketchup can stain your shirt, so use those paper napkins. Loud and boisterous behavior might ruin someone else's picnic, so keep a lid on things.

To make a good picnic a great picnic, consider the following choices:

✦ **Ants can ruin the best picnic**, so if you spill some food, clean it up. That will cut back on the chance of an ant invasion.

✦ **Once you get sand in your food, you can never get it out,** so don't run or roughhouse around food (yours or someone else's).

✦ **Broken glass is a danger** to picnickers and others, so if you break something, clean it up completely!

✦ **People have different tastes in music,** so don't play your favorite songs so loud that everyone else in the park has to listen.

✦ The lifeguards and rangers are there to work, so **follow their instructions** and don't be disappointed if they don't accept your offers to join your picnic.

✦ The beauty of the parks and beaches depends on how clean they are, so **don't litter, and do help clean up when you are done.**

If everyone makes good choices, the beaches and parks will be the sites of fun and delicious picnics for years to come.

BUFFETS

Whether you are at a dinner party at someone's home, a restaurant, or a special dinner at school, you may find yourself at a "buffet." A buffet is where all the food for the meal is set out in serving platters on a big table; the plates are in a stack at one end, and each person passes by the table and serves himself just what he wants. In some buffets there are servers who will put just the foods you ask for onto your plate.

In restaurants and cafeterias, health laws require a protective shield over buffet lines to keep people from breathing and coughing on the food. The shields are set high enough so you can reach under them with your hands and they are made of clear glass or plastic so you can see what you are serving yourself, but the shield protects the food from germs you or other diners might spread. At private parties or celebrations there are no shields, so it is important not to breathe directly on food and to step away from the line if you need to cough.

One of the positive points about buffets is that you are usually welcome to return as often as you like and serve yourself some more food—so you do not need to overload your plate the first time around. In a restaurant, simply leave your used plate at your table and get a clean one in order to get more food. While you are at the buffet table, your waiter will clear your used plate. At a

LINE MANNERS REVISITED

Sometimes there is a line at the buffet table, so remember your line manners. As they say, "Patience is a virtue."

private party or celebration you may just return to the buffet table with your plate and get some more food.

At some buffets there will be separate tables for salads and desserts. Each of those tables will have clean plates for you. The same manners apply at the salad and dessert tables: If you have to cough, step out of line; don't pile all those desserts on your plate; if there are servers, be sure to thank them and smile.

POTLUCK

PICTURE THIS: Every year there is a neighborhood supper at the community center. Everyone brings a dish of food. One year, everyone brings desserts. What can you do?

The only thing is to enjoy a whole dinner of dessert. That's why it's called potluck. Sometimes everyone brings pasta dishes or salads, and that's what you get. It's part of the fun!

At a potluck supper all the dishes are served buffet style. The guests file past the table, serving themselves a spoonful of anything that looks delicious to them. Potlucks usually work out remarkably well. The variety of meals (even when they are all of one type) insures that there is something everyone can enjoy.

Beyond the table manners that would be important at any meal, it is important at a potluck to not make negative comments about the food as you pass by the table. The person who cooked it might just be in line behind you and may be offended by an "Ewwww—what's that? It looks gross!" While that would not be polite in *any* setting, there's a higher risk of hurting someone's feelings if it's at a potluck.

Once you have filled your plate with food, find a place to sit. Sometimes there will be tables and chairs to choose from, sometimes the only option is the regular living-room or outdoor furniture, and sometimes you may just find a comfortable place on the floor. Remember all your best eating manners, have some great conversation with friends or family, and enjoy the great variety (the real advantage of a potluck) of food you now have on your plate.

At most potlucks everyone is responsible for bringing some food and taking his or her dish home to wash it *or* for helping clean the dishes at the community center, school, house of worship, or host's house. The real point of a potluck is to share the work of food preparation, serving, and cleaning up. So join in, any way you can!

SPECIAL CELEBRATIONS AND HOLIDAYS

Whether the special event is a wedding, graduation, birthday, or holiday, you may be feeling a little nervous about what you might have to do or eat! Sometimes these occasions come packed with their own types of table manners, which might seem confusing. Maybe there will be foods that are new and different to you. Perhaps you will be faced with more utensils than you've ever imagined possible! Not to worry: You can enjoy special occasions without letting all of those forks or the fancy dishes and foods bother you. Here are some things you might experience, and some easy ways for dealing with them:

Special foods: Over time, traditions have developed that associate certain foods with celebratory or holiday meals.

Thanksgiving: turkey and pumpkin pie

Fourth of July: fried chicken or barbecue

Labor Day: corned beef boiled dinner

Birthday: Ask the birthday girl or boy.

JUST THE TWO OF YOU

*W*hen you and your best friend are at the dinner table, remember there are other people there too. If you giggle and whisper throughout the meal, others may think they are the subject of your joke or they may feel left out. A holiday or celebration meal is a social event for the whole family. You can help make it successful by participating and being part of the whole group.

Different religious and ethnic holidays may have specific foods that are symbolic to the day. If you have grown up in the tradition, you will be familiar with and look forward to what will be served. If you are visiting and celebrating with a friend and the tradition is not your own, you may want to talk to your parent or another adult about the day and what you can expect. Once you are at the celebration, offer to help out with the preparations. Not only will your help be appreciated by your host, you'll become familiar with what the table will look like and what foods are going to be served. If you have questions, ask your friend. And once you are seated at the meal, just wait until you see what the others at the table do and then follow their example.

Special people: Who will be attending? Whether at a family celebration or a special meal at a friend's home, there may be people coming whom you do not know very well. In addition to reviewing how to make small talk (see Chapter Four, pages 63–64), here are some tips for easy and enjoyable mealtime conversations when you are in an unfamiliar setting:

✦ **Learn the names of people you don't know—**a big part of good table manners.

✦ **Think about the last time you saw these people.** You can ask about things that have happened since the last holiday together.

✦ **What are some things *you* have been doing?** Perhaps you can tell them about the special award in theater your school just won—and your part in that musical.

Special family, religious, and cultural traditions: Some families watch football games before and after the Thanksgiving meal. Others say grace at the start of every meal, and maybe there are additional prayers in recognition of a religious holiday that is being celebrated. What do you do if you're a visitor in someone's home and you're unfamiliar with their customs? A good guest is interested in what is happening and is a courteous observer or participant. You should show your respect by remaining quiet during a prayer, even if your hosts celebrate a religion other than your own. You make others feel good when you want to learn about their customs. For instance, if you're attending a Passover meal, you can ask, "Why do you eat matzo during Passover?" Your host might enjoy telling you that this unleavened bread is eaten because the Jewish people ate it when they fled Egypt.

You should show your respect by remaining quiet during a prayer, even if your hosts celebrate a religion other than your own.

THE CELEBRATION HAS ENDED

Dessert is over and all the food is gone. Some people may be lingering over their cup of coffee, but others have begun to clear the table. This is the same the world around, and just like you would do at home, you can offer to help clear. The host may not accept your offer, but it will be much appreciated. Thank-yous—to your hosts, the chef, and those who helped with the meal— are all in order.

While it is not required, you could write a short thank-you note and mail

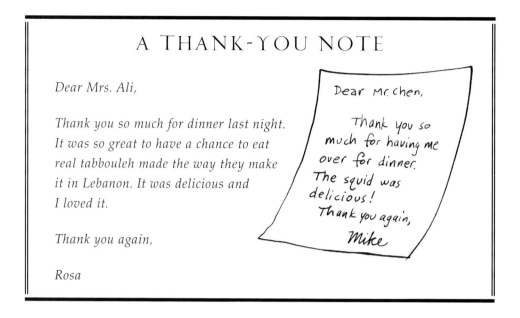

A THANK-YOU NOTE

Dear Mrs. Ali,

Thank you so much for dinner last night.
It was so great to have a chance to eat
real tabbouleh made the way they make
it in Lebanon. It was delicious and
I loved it.

Thank you again,

Rosa

Dear Mr. Chen,

Thank you so
much for having me
over for dinner.
The squid was
delicious!
Thank you again,

Mike

it the very next day. Two or three sentences are all it takes, and you will make someone's day!

AWARDS CEREMONIES AND . . .

There are times when the eating is over, but no one gets up from the table. For instance, most schools have sports awards ceremonies at the end of each season. Dinner may be a potluck, a buffet, or a sit-down affair, depending on the school and the formality of the event. After everyone is finished eating, people push their chairs back and face the stage or lectern at the front of the room, and the speeches and awards begin.

Whether it is an awards ceremony, a dinner theater, or another type of event, the important thing is to change the focus of your attention from mealtime manners to audience manners. While you are still at the table— maybe even still eating dessert—it is important to behave in a way that is respectful and considerate of those who are part of the program. You can keep your conversation to a minimum—speak only in between awards or acts. If you need to go to the restroom, excuse yourself and head right out of the hall. When you return, wait until there is a break in the program to go to your table. If you are part of the program, follow the instructions given by the adults in charge. If you are being given an award, be sure to have an appropriate thank-you ready, speak clearly, keep it short, and, most of all, enjoy yourself.

ETHNIC DINING

Chinese food—maybe it's your favorite! How about sushi? Or, for some of you, it might be Italian or Indian or Middle Eastern. You may find yourself in a situation where the food being served is completely new to you. Many foods, spices, and herbs are an acquired taste, so don't be surprised if you don't like everything. It's polite to try at least a little of everything, but you don't have to finish it all. You certainly may ask what things are, but be careful not to react negatively. If someone says, "Oh, that's eel," and eel is not something you have eaten before, you don't want to say, "Ewww!" Instead, simply say, "No thank you, I think I'll try this other dish."

Some ethnic food is supposed to be eaten with your fingers. Watch your hosts and see if they break off a piece of their pita bread and dip it into the small dishes on the table or put some of the food

Boiled goat head? Sounds...interesting. I'll try a little bit.

directly onto the pita bread with a knife or spreader. Follow their lead and you will be fine. Just as you can ask what ingredients are in the dish in front of you, you can ask how to eat it correctly.

If you can use chopsticks, by all means do. If you don't know how, ask for a fork or, better yet, ask someone to show you how to use the chopsticks correctly. If you know you are going to a meal that is traditionally eaten with chopsticks, try them out at home and practice, to hone your skills. (See Chapter Two, pages 38–39.) Some of the fun of eating foods from different cultures is to learn the traditional way of eating them. Sometimes kung pao chicken may actually taste better if you eat it with chopsticks.

CHAPTER SIX

BEYOND TABLE MANNERS: WHEN YOU'RE THE HOST

Knowing which fork to use, how to start a conversation, or what to do when you need to sneeze are all important table manners skills. Whatever the occasion, they are essential to an enjoyable meal. But being a great host goes beyond basic table manners to making guests feel relaxed and welcome. Guests should have such a good time, they'll want to come back again and again. In this chapter we'll explore what it takes to be a gracious host.

Being a host involves serving a meal or refreshments of some sort that you plan, prepare, and clean up! The best idea is to start small—both in numbers of guests and amount of food. Try having some friends over for lunch, serving peanut butter and jelly sandwiches, chips, carrot sticks, and a "build your own ice-cream sundae" buffet. Or you could host a sleepover pizza party and a cold cereal breakfast the next day. If you are allowed to use the stove (or if your mom or dad can give you a hand), you can try something more ambitious, like pancakes. The possibilities are endless, but you need to take into account your age, your abilities, and the kind of food you and your guests would enjoy. Then—once the choice is made—the number-one thing is to plan, plan, plan.

FIRST THINGS FIRST

Even though it's your party, it is important to show consideration and respect for your parents and anyone else in your family who might use the kitchen and family space you need to entertain your friends. Talk over your ideas with your parents. Before you do too much planning, make certain that your ideas are doable and that your parents have agreed with you about

- ✦ **The date and time;**
- ✦ **The type of party;**
- ✦ **The guest list;**
- ✦ **The food you will serve and your plans for preparing it;**
- ✦ **Any other activities you have planned.**

These are all the key ingredients for a successful party.

THE DATE AND TIME

PICTURE THIS: You have planned an awesome party. Your parents are going to help you with preparing a special meal. You have a DVD of the best concert given by your favorite group. You're inviting five of your closest friends. But then, when you call them all, you discover four of them can't even come because they are singing in a concert with the school chorus (you don't sing and didn't even know about the concert!).

Give careful thought to the selection of the day and the time for your party. Consider the school calendar, holidays, or special events that happen in your community. All these things can create a dilemma for your friends who will want to come to your party but may be committed to something else.

When you decide on your time frame, don't forget to give an ending time. This lets your guests know when they should plan for a ride home. Also, if there is no end time noted, your guests just might stay on, and on, and on, and on. . . . When people know what's expected of them, they tend to enjoy the party more. It eliminates guesswork that can be a little disconcerting for both the host and the guest!

THE TYPE OF PARTY

> *Whatever the type of party, your job as host is to make sure your guests enjoy themselves.*

Here's where you put your imagination and creativity to work. The decision about the type of food to serve depends on what type of party it will be. Are you getting a group of friends together to eat takeout and then go to a movie? Are you planning some outdoor activity like a hike to a local hilltop that's capped off with a picnic with a view? Maybe you'll invite a group of friends over who love the same kind of music you do and they each will bring their favorite playlist and a snack. Or . . . maybe the party will revolve around food where the main activity is the meal. Whatever the type of party, your job as host is to make sure your guests enjoy themselves.

THE GUEST LIST

Whatever type of party you plan, one of the main ingredients for success is the guest list. Answering the questions "How many?" and "Who?" has always been a major challenge for hosts. A fun supper for a few friends may mean just four or six guests. A bring-your-best-healthy-snack-and-playlist party could mean ten or twelve guests. Once you've decided "how many," you're ready to think about "who?"

Some things to consider:

✦ **Having decided what type of party,** consider which of your friends would enjoy it. If you are planning a party where the main activity will be a picnic and a volleyball game, you'll only want to invite friends who love volleyball.

✦ **Who gets along with whom?** You don't want to invite two people you know don't really like each other—even if you really like them both. Make a choice to invite one, and then invite the other to your next party.

✦ **Could this be an opportunity to get to know some new people?** Maybe you don't want to invite only your very best friends. If you're having a party for eight or nine kids, you might want to invite some of the kids you haven't gotten to know that well at school too.

A great guest list brings together a group of people who can enjoy one another's company. It's not easy; it takes practice. But you can do it.

THE FOOD YOU WILL SERVE AND YOUR PLANS FOR PREPARING IT

Next, you get to choose the menu! Here are three key questions to ask yourself:

1. What type of food do you like?

2. What type of food can you cook?

3. How much time and help will you have to prepare it?

Start with yourself. You may spend a fair amount of time preparing the food, so choose something you really like. Also, consider your guests. It's best not to prepare something with a really unusual taste or lots of spice. Just because you like extra-hot salsa doesn't mean all your guests will like it, too!

You also need to plan something you can prepare. What is your experience with cooking? Does your menu require the use of the stove? Are you allowed to use the stove? Are the ingredients ones that are readily available? Have you made these dishes before? How complicated are they? All these questions will help you choose a menu that you can call your own. Planning a party that requires your mom or dad to cook and serve food for you doesn't count. The idea is to learn how to balance all the activities of hosting a party on your own—and that includes the actual cooking!

DO A TEST RUN

It's a good rule of thumb to prepare any dish on your menu at least once before you try it out on guests. OR, if you can't do that, only experiment on people who love you. That way, if things go awry, you are in the most forgiving group possible, and your serving of a less-than-perfect dish will have you all laughing in years to come.

ANY ACTIVITIES YOU HAVE PLANNED?

Some activities, by their very nature, will require adult assistance. If you all are going somewhere away from the home, you may need help with transportation. If you're planning a barbecue at your pool, you'll need parents' approval and adult supervision. Talk with your parents about both the need

THE GREAT HOST

1. Plans carefully for every aspect of his party.

2. Includes date, time, location, directions (if needed), and any special information on the invitation, so guests will know what is expected of them.

3. Asks guests if there are any foods they cannot eat.

4. Prepares everything possible before guests arrive.

5. Greets every guest with a smile and a hello when they arrive.

6. Makes sure everyone is included in the conversation and activities.

7. Is available to say good-bye and thanks every guest for coming as they leave.

for assistance and what you all consider to be good supervision. Parents don't need to take part in the activities, but they do need to have a presence. So work it out with them ahead of time so everyone knows what the expectations are.

Choices about activities weave in and out with the food choices you make. How much time do you have? How much time will it take to finish eating? How much time will the activities require? How much time do you want to just socialize with your friends? If you are having friends over for a sit-down meal, that may be your major activity and you may not need to even plan much else.

IT'S PARTY TIME

A QUESTION *for* CINDY & PEGGY

QUESTION: *Last week I held my first dinner party. I invited five friends over for a Mexican dinner (chicken fajitas, rice and beans, and salad). They all had a wonderful time talking in the living room. I spent the whole time in the kitchen. They all say it was a great party, but I never had a chance to enjoy it. What should I have done?*

ANSWER: *Plan, plan, plan—then—prepare, prepare, prepare! The measure of a great party is one where the host can actually enjoy it along with her guests.*

This is easy to do if you plan a meal that can be made earlier in the day. Salads can be made ahead of time and kept cold in the refrigerator. The filling for the fajitas and the rice and beans can be prepared ahead of time and kept warm so that all the host has to do is warm up the tortillas and serve them. That only takes a few minutes.

Or . . . the host can invite everyone to join her in the kitchen so she can be part of the party as she makes the final preparations. Then, everyone can go together to the table when the meal is ready.

In either case, the host should have the table set, glasses out, and beverages ready to serve before the guests arrive. These tips are for any meal—not just a formal dinner. Plan ahead, prepare ahead, and you will enjoy your party along with your guests.

THE PARTY'S OVER, OR IS IT?

Everyone has headed home. You are exhausted. You have spent all day preparing for it and you've been cooking, greeting, talking, serving food, talking, serving more food, talking, and sending people on their way. You look

around. There are dishes in the sink, chairs to be moved back to their places, food to be put away, and trash to be taken out. The party really isn't over. When you are the host, it's your job to clean up. So put on your favorite music or television show, kick off your shoes, and get to it. In the morning, when you want to sleep in, you'll be glad you did.

Entertaining is something you'll do many times and in many ways. The pleasure is in repeating the successes and fixing those things that may not have been perfect the last time. You've had a chance to try out your table manners, your cooking ability, your social skills, and what it takes to host a party. Before you play in a soccer tournament or piano concert, you practice your skills. It's the same with hosting.

It's not always easy, but entertaining brings huge rewards. The time we spend with friends is so special—and sharing food with them can be the most special time of all. It takes planning, caring, paying attention, consideration, and, of course, the best table manners. But put all these elements together and your friends will treasure your invitations and look forward to the next party you host.

It's not always easy, but entertaining brings huge rewards.

INDEX